# He Reserves Wrath For His Enemies

## An Open Letter To Born-again, Bible-believing Christians

HARRISON HOUSE
Tulsa, Oklahoma

Mission To America
736 Wilson Road
Humble, Texas 77338

ISBN 0-89274-229-1

Published by Harrison House, Inc.
P. O. Box 35035
Tulsa, Oklahoma 74135

Printed in the United States of America

**Let's talk about God's wrath . . .**

If you and I were now having a discussion about your wrath, your anger, your indignation, I would have to let you specify what makes you mad. In fact, if I were to start sounding off as an expert in what makes you mad, the only thing I would probably accomplish is to make you mad.

Similarly, we must let God specify what His wrath is, when it can be expected, and against whom it will be directed. Those who think God is only love and nothing more need to spend more time reading the Bible. Consider this:

*Who can stand before His indignation? And who can stand up and endure the fierceness of His anger? His wrath is poured out like fire, and the rocks are broken asunder by Him.*

*Nahum* 1:6

Soon after the Lord God spoke these words through His prophet Nahum, He utterly destroyed the city of Nineveh.

God's indignation . . . His anger . . . His wrath.

If we approach the Bible prayerfully and with a mind open to the teachings of the Holy Spirit, we'll understand more and more of this side of God — of what His wrath is and, most importantly, who will suffer and be destroyed under it.

**Who will be destroyed?**

*. . . the Lord takes vengeance on His adversaries and reserves wrath for His enemies.*

*Nahum 1:2*

*Reserves.* When something is reserved, it is set apart for future use, set apart for a particular person.

**For whom does God reserve His wrath?** His enemies.

**Who are His enemies?**

*Do you not know that being the world's friend is being God's enemy? So whoever chooses to be a friend of the world takes his stand as an enemy of God.*

*James 4:4*

But read what Jesus says about us:

*No one has greater love — no one has shown stronger affection — than to lay down (give up) his own life for his friends.*

*You are My friends, if you keep on doing the things which I command you to do.*

*I do not call you servants (slaves) any longer, for the servant does not know what his master is doing (working out). But I have called you My friends, because I have made known to you everything that I have heard from My Father — I have revealed to you everything that I have learned from Him.*

*John 15:13-15*

Jesus gave up His life for His friends; and one of the things He has revealed to every born-again believer, including you, is that He gave up His life for you.

If you accept that He gave up His life for you, then you are His friend. If you are His friend (and by the authority of His Word you are!), then you are not His enemy.

*For God has not appointed us to [incur His] wrath . . . .*

*1 Thessalonians 5:9*

*The Living Bible* sets it forth beautifully in these two verses:

"For God sent Christ Jesus to take the punishment for our sins and to end all God's anger against us. He used Christ's blood and our faith as the means of saving us from his wrath."

Romans 3:25

". . . Now he will save us from all of God's wrath to come."

Romans 5:9

We would do well to memorize this last verse: **He** will save us from **all** of God's wrath **to come.**

**But who will be the recipients of God's wrath?**

Read what the Apostle Paul wrote:

*. . . Are you unmindful or actually ignorant [of the fact] that God's kindness is intended to lead you to repent — to change your mind and inner man to accept God's will?*

*But by your callous stubbornness and impenitence of heart you are storing up wrath and indignation for yourself on the day of wrath and indignation, when God's righteous judgment (just doom) will be revealed.*

*Romans 2:4,5*

Are you impenitent and stubborn, living in rebellion against God's will and refusing to repent? No? Then you are not one of those who is storing up wrath and indignation for himself on the day of wrath and indignation.

**But what is this "day of wrath"?**

One good definition of it is found in Revelation, chapter 6, a capsule description of the Great Tribulation known as "The Book of the Wrath of God."

Paul further describes those who bring upon themselves God's wrath. Can the following be a description of a born-again, Bible-believing child of God?

*But for those who are self-seeking and self-willed and disobedient to the*

*Truth but responsive to wickedness, there will be indignation and wrath.*

*Romans 2:8*

**Is the Great Tribulation the wrath of God?**

It is the result of the end-time pouring out of the wrath of God upon all who dwell on the earth. The Bible makes that clear. But let's be sure to understand one thing: the wrath of God is not limited to the Great Tribulation. However, we born-again followers of the Lord Jesus Christ will not experience everything that the Bible defines as God's wrath.

**But is the rapidly approaching seven-year Tribulation Period really defined by God's Word as the wrath of God?**

Judge for yourself:

*Then the kings of the earth and their noblemen and their magnates and their military chiefs and the wealthy and the strong and [everyone, whether] slave or free, hid themselves in the caves and among the rocks of the mountains,*

*And they called to the mountains and the rocks, Fall on (before) us and hide us from the face of Him Who sits on the throne, and from the deep-seated indignation and wrath of the Lamb.*

*For the great day of His wrath (vengeance, retribution, indignation) has come, and who is able to stand before it?*

Revelation 6:15-17

Who indeed? But there's more to tell us that the Tribulation Period is a great outpouring of the wrath of God. Read the description of the seven plagues in Revelation:

*. . . There were seven angels bringing seven plagues (afflictions, calamities), which are the last, for with them God's wrath (indignation) is completely expressed — reaches its climax and is ended.*

Revelation 15:1

*And one of the four living creatures [then] gave the seven angels seven bowls of gold full of the wrath and indignation of God . . . .*

Revelation 15:7

*Then I heard a mighty voice from the temple sanctuary saying to the seven angels, Go and empty out on the earth the seven bowls of God's wrath and indignation.*

*Revelation 16:1*

The prophet Isaiah had plenty to say about the Great Tribulation. For example:

*Behold, the day of the Lord comes! Fierce, with wrath and raging anger, to make the land and the whole earth a desolation, and to destroy out of it its sinners.*

*Isaiah 13:9*

*Therefore I will make the heavens tremble, and the earth shall be shaken out of its place at the wrath of the Lord of hosts in the day of His fierce anger.*

*Isaiah 13:13*

Let's look at another Old Testament description of an example of the wrath of God. The prophet Ezekiel, in chapters 38 and 39, describes a devastating war that will soon take place:

*And the word of the Lord came to me:*

*Son of man, set your face against Gog, of the land of Magog, the prince of Rosh, of Meshech, and Tubal, and prophesy against him.*

Ezekiel 38:1,2

**But who is this Gog? Where does he come from?**

*And you* (Gog) *will come from your place out of the uttermost parts of the north . . . .*

Ezekiel 38:15

**The uttermost parts of the north? That can't be Turkey. It must be Russia!**

Indeed, Moscow (Meshech) is directly north of Jerusalem. Tubal today is Tobolsk in Siberia; Rosh is Russia.

**When will this war with Russia take place?**

*. . . in the latter years you shall go against the land that is restored from the ravages of the sword, where people*

*are gathered out of many nations upon the mountains of Israel, which had been a continual waste; but its [people] are brought forth out of the nations, and they shall dwell securely, all of them.*

*Ezekiel 38:8*

So this war will take place in the latter years (that's now) after the rebirth of Israel (which we've all seen) when its people are living in peace.

**What? Peace in the Middle East?**

Yes. Read Ezekiel 38:11,14.

Some people believe that Ezekiel, chapters 38 and 39, describe the Battle of Armageddon, but that isn't so. Even though there is divine intervention in both battles, there are enough differences to prove that they are two separate and distinct battles. Two major differences are:

**Opposing Forces.** Ezekiel describes a massive attack launched by Russia and her allies against Israel. Although there are descriptions of activities seven months after the battle (39:12) and seven years after the battle (39:9), no mention is made of the return of Jesus or the binding of Satan.

In the Battle of Armageddon, the armies of the revived ten-nation Beast System join forces with the 200,000,000-man Oriental army to make war against the Lord Jesus Christ and His army. (Rev. 19:14.) At that time, the Lord Jesus Christ is returning to the earth, and we are returning with Him. (Zech. 14:5; Rev. 17:14.) The Battle ends with the defeat of the Antichrist and the False Prophet, with the utter destruction of their armies, and with the binding of Satan.

**Location.** The armies of Gog and his allies are destroyed in the mountains and the fields in the north of Israel. (Ezek. 39:4,5.) But the Battle of Armageddon takes place in the Valley of Megiddo, which extends from the Plain of Jezreel to the outskirts of Jerusalem.

That the wrath of God is involved is crystal clear.

*But in that day when Gog shall come against the land of Israel, says the Lord God, My wrath shall come up into My nostrils. For in My jealousy and in the fire of My wrath . . . .*

*Ezekiel 38:18,19*

**And what will the wrath of God bring about?**

The utter, complete destruction of Russia and her allies. Horrible, total destruction. Isn't that always the result of the wrath of God?

**But what does all this have to do with the Tribulation Period?**

The key is at the end of Ezekiel 39:9:

*And [when you, Gog, are no longer] they who dwell in the cities of Israel shall go forth, and shall set on fire and burn the battle gear, the shields and the bucklers, the bows and the arrows, the handspikes or riding whips and the spears, and they shall burn them as fuel for seven years.*

**Seven years? Is that seven-year period significant?**

It sure is! What seven-year period does the Bible teach will occur after the Jews have been gathered out of all the nations and the land of Israel restored? The Tribulation Period, the Time of Jacob's Trouble. Could Ezekiel 39:9 be referring to any other seven-year period yet to take place? If so, it is not mentioned anywhere else in God's Word. There is one, and only one, seven-year period yet to take place.

This seven-year period is the Tribulation, and this war against Russia occurs at the very beginning of the Tribulation. Remember that the prophet Daniel, chapter 9, verse 24, defined 70 weeks of years of God's determined dealings with Israel. (The Tribulation is the 70th week.)

Read Ezekiel 38 and 39. Understand the horrible, total destruction soon to fall upon Russia and her allies. Think about it. Then answer this question: *What about the born-again Christians in Russia?*

**Do the promises of God apply to them as they apply to us?**

They most certainly do!

**Do the Russian Christians have the same right we have to rely on the Rapture of the Church by Jesus to save them from the wrath of God?**

Yes! Yes! Yes! Praise God!

The facts are these: Ezekiel 38:18,19 define the conquest and devastation of Russia and her allies as a result of the wrath of God. But He reserves wrath for his enemies and the Russian Christians are His friends, His children, just as we are.

Therefore, by the authority of the precious Word of God, the Russian Christians will be taken out of Russia before the wrath of God destroys it, just as Lot was taken out of Sodom. The Russian Christians will not be around for the utter destruction of Russia any more than we will.

By the way, Ezekiel 39:22 describes why this war will take place. To understand what that will lead to, read Romans 11:25,26 and see how beautifully it all fits together.

**Is there the possibility that the wrath of God poured out during the Tribulation will hit some people but not others?**

What did Jesus say?

*For it will come upon all who live upon the face of the entire earth.*

*Luke 21:35*

Yet somehow the Lord God will protect three groups of people from His wrath during the Tribulation. (Praise God that we won't be around to learn how He will do this!) The three groups are all His people:

1. the 144,000 young Jewish evangelists.
2. their converts.
3. the protector of the Israelites.

It will be an eerie day when the 144,000 are sealed. We read about it in Revelation, chapter 7:

*After this I saw four angels stationed at the four corners of the earth, firmly holding back the four winds of the earth, so that no wind should blow on the earth or sea or upon any tree.*

*Then I saw a second angel coming up from the east (the rising of the sun), and carrying the seal of the living God. And with a loud voice he called out to the four angels who had been given authority and power to injure earth and sea,*

*Saying, Harm neither the earth nor the sea nor the trees, until we have sealed the bond servants of our God upon their foreheads.*

*And [then] I heard how many were sealed (marked) out of every tribe of the sons of Israel; there were a hundred and forty-four thousand sealed.*

*Revelation 7:1-4*

Have you read of the horrible insects from the bottomless pit that torment mankind for five terrible months during the Tribulation? They are described in Revelation 9:1-11. Pay particular attention to verse 4, and you'll see that they were not permitted to attack those people with the seal of God on their foreheads. The prophet Ezekiel teaches us that those with the seal of God will be divinely protected, not only from demonic insects, but from all else in the Tribulation:

> *And the Lord said to him, Go through the midst of the city, through the midst of Jerusalem, and set a mark upon the foreheads of the men who sigh and groan over all the abominations that are committed in the midst of it.*
>
> *And to the others He said in my hearing, Follow [the man with the ink bottle] through the city, and smite; let not your eye spare, neither have any pity.*
>
> *Slay outright the elderly, the young man and the virgin, the infant and the women; but do not touch or go near any one on whom is the mark . . . .*
>
> Ezekiel 9:4-6

For another description of righteous men living in a land upon which the wrath of God has come, read Ezekiel 14:13-20. Once again, God spares His people. The protector of Israel will be protected because of the unbreakable promise of Genesis 12:3, in which the Lord states that He will bless those who bless Abraham (and his descendants). To befriend the Jews is to gain God's promise of sure reward.

**Who is the protector of the Israelites?**

It is a nation, the same nation who is the sponsor of the tiny nation of Israel: the United States of America. Our nation has always opened its doors to the Jewish people. During the Tribulation, the Antichrist will bring terrible persecution on the Israelites, and many of them will flee to America for protection. America may come through the Tribulation chastened, but many will repent and turn to God after the Church has been raptured, and these Tribulation saints will be ushered into the Millennium at Christ's return.

The pre-Tribulation Rapture of the Church, plus the protection of Tribulation saints while God's judgment is being poured out on the entire earth, is not new in scripture. It was revealed to us in type and prefigure in Genesis, chapters 5-9.

With Seth began the righteous lineage of Adam and Eve. His descendant Enoch walked in faith and fellowship with God and was raptured.

**When?**

Before the worldwide flood. (See Gen. 5:24 and Heb. 11:5.) According to Jude, verses 14 and 15, Enoch had been warning the people of a coming judgment. But it was a judgment in which he himself never participated because God translated him to heaven before the judgment came. Enoch typifies the Church.

Later, Noah preached righteousness to the people. (2 Pet. 2:5.) The Holy Spirit strived with them. (Gen. 6:3.) They were without excuse. Then the Flood came, and Noah and his family were borne up over it in safety, in the ark. Noah and his family typify those who will be protected during the Tribulation.

In Matthew 24:37-41, the Lord Jesus compared the days just before the Flood with the days just before the Tribulation. Have you compared the days just before the Flood with today? If so, you've discovered how very similar the "days of Noah" are with today. The Lord had more to say about this. He addressed the following to the Church:

*Keep awake then and watch at all times (that is, be discreet, attentive and ready); praying that you may have the full strength and ability and be accounted worthy to escape all these things [taken together] that will take place, and to stand in the presence of the Son of man.*

*Luke 21:36*

Let's examine this scripture in reverse order. We are to pray that we will stand in the presence of the Son of Man. Before we do that, we should know where He is!

**Where is the Son of Man right now? And where will He be during the Tribulation?**

Acts 3:20,21 tells us that He is now in heaven. Revelation, chapter 6, shows Him in heaven during the Tribulation Period, opening the seven seals. The Son of Man is now in heaven and will remain there until His glorious return at the end of the Tribulation. If we are to stand in His presence during the Tribulation, it will have to be in heaven.

**What are "all these things (taken together) that will take place"?**

The Tribulation!

**And what about that word "escape"?**

Look it up, if you must. The angels told Lot to "escape" (Gen. 19:17) from Sodom before destruction from God came. In addition, one of the angels told Lot that he was unable to call down destruction on Sodom until Lot had safely made his escape. (Gen. 19:22.)

**The Lord said, ". . . and be accounted worthy to escape." What about that?**

Please note that to be *accounted worthy* is not the same thing as to be worthy. That word *accounted* is there for a reason. You and I could never get anywhere on our own worthiness, but we are accounted worthy when we have His worthiness. The Lord Jesus Christ imparts His worthiness to us to make us worthy.

*This is positive proof of the just and right judgment of God to the end that you may be deemed deserving of His kingdom — a plain token of His fair verdict [which designs] that you should be made and counted worthy of the kingdom of God — for the sake of which you are also suffering.*

*2 Thessalonians 1:5*

*Not that we are fit (qualified and sufficient in ability) of ourselves to form personal judgments or to claim or count anything as coming from us; but our power and ability and sufficiency are from God.*

*[It is He] Who has qualified us (making us to be fit and worthy and sufficient) as ministers and dispensers of a new covenant . . . .*

*2 Corinthians 3:5,6*

*But if one loves God truly — with affectionate reverence, prompt obedience and grateful recognition of His blessing — he is known by God [that is, recognized as worthy of His intimacy and love, and he is owned by Him].*

*1 Corinthians 8:3*

Read Luke 20:35,36. Then determine who are the sons of God to which James refers. If you are a born-again believer, then you are one of them — one of *those who are considered worthy.*

We thank You, beloved Lord Jesus, that we, the Church, are accounted worthy to escape these things that will soon come to pass. We thank You for Your worthiness. Worthy is the Lamb that was slain! Oh, how we love You and praise You, O Lamb of God!

*In My Father's house there are many dwelling places (homes). If it were not so, I would have told you, for I am going away to prepare a place for you.*

*And when (if) I go and make ready a place for you, I will come back again and will take you to Myself, that where I am you may be also.*

*John 14:2,3*

**Why do some believe the Church is going through the Tribulation?**

Some people read Matthew 24 and conclude that the Church is going through the Tribulation. They have not examined the whole of God's Word. Don't limit your reading to Matthew 24 unless you feel that Luke 21, Mark 13, and all the many other applicable scriptures are somehow less valid than Matthew 24.

I've heard people read Matthew 24:31 (which takes place at the end of the Tribulation) and say triumphantly, "See! That's the Rapture!" It says:

*And He will send out His angels with a loud trumpet call, and they will gather His elect [His chosen ones] from the four winds, [even] from one end of the universe to the other.*

*Matthew 24:31*

There's another description of the same thing in Mark's Gospel:

*And then He will send out the angels and will gather together His elect — those He has picked out for Himself — from the four winds, from the farthest bounds of the earth to the farthest bounds of heaven.*

*Mark 13:27*

As we take these two descriptions together (so that we may believe the whole of God's Word), we see that at the Lord's command His angels gather us together, both from the earth and from heaven.

Well, if that is the Rapture of the Church, then the Bible contradicts itself. Another Scripture passage says:

*For the Lord Himself will descend from heaven with a loud cry of summons, with the shout of an archangel, and with the blast of the trumpet of God. And those who have departed this life in Christ will rise first.*

*Then we, the still living who remain [on the earth], shall simultaneously be caught up along with (the resurrected dead) in the clouds to meet the Lord in the air; and so always — through the eternity of the eternities — we shall be with the Lord!*

*1 Thessalonians 4:16,17*

We Bible-believing children of God know that our Lord does not contradict Himself. He is not confused. There is no possibility whatever that Jesus Christ cannot make up His mind about whether His angels or He Himself will gather us.

Other differences are equally obvious. The dead *and* the living take part in the Rapture, but the dead are not mentioned in Matthew 24:31 and Mark 13:27, which describe an angelic gathering of believers from heaven and earth. The Rapture is limited to the earth; no gathering of believers in heaven is mentioned.

Bible-believing Christians can only conclude that Matthew 24:31 and Mark 13:27 are not descriptions of the Rapture of the Church occurring at the end of the Tribulation. Rather, they are descriptions of the angelic gathering of

Tribulation saints (who are *not* the Church) and the Church to return with Him to reign with Him for 1,000 years.

**By the way, who are the "elect" spoken of in Matthew 24 (especially Matt. 24:31 above) and Mark 13?**

In the context in which it is presented to us, the word *elect* refers primarily to the elect of Israel who are now free to join the elect (the Church) returning from heaven to participate in the glorious Millennium.

**But there are people who insist that the word "elect" refers only to the Church. They'll show you scripture after scripture in which the word "elect" does indeed refer to the Church. What about that?**

Read Isaiah 42:1-7. It's a beautiful prophecy that looks ahead to our Lord Jesus. Note that verse 1 refers to Jesus as "My Servant . . . My elect." God's Holy Word uses *elect* to refer to more than only His Church. This is also true in Isaiah 65, verses 9 and 22. And why not? We are all His elect in Christ, and Christ is the Elect of God! Praise God!

*Take notice! I tell you a mystery — a secret truth, an event decreed by the hidden purpose or counsel of God. We shall not all fall asleep [in death], but we shall all be changed (transformed)*

*In a moment, in the twinkling of an eye, at the (sound of the) last trumpet call. For a trumpet will sound, and the dead [in Christ] will be raised imperishable — free and immune from decay — and we shall be changed (transformed).*

*1 Corinthians 15:51,52*

Some say that this proves the Church will go through the Tribulation, because the "last trumpet call" is the seventh trumpet of the Book of Revelation.

If it is, the Word of God contradicts itself. What did the other description of the Rapture say about that trumpet?

*For the Lord Himself will descend from heaven with a loud cry of summons, with the shout of an archangel, and with the blast of the trumpet of God . . . .*

*1 Thessalonians 4:16*

But the trumpets referred to in Revelation are angelic trumpets, and trumpets of woe, not joy, for those who dwell upon the face of the earth:

*Then I saw the seven angels who stand before God, and to them were given seven trumpets.*

Revelation 8:2

*Then the seven angels who had the seven trumpets prepared to sound them.*

Revelation 8:6

*. . . Woe, woe, woe to those who dwell on the earth, because of the rest of the trumpet blasts which the three angels are about to sound!*

Revelation 8:13

*But when the days come that the trumpet call of the seventh angel is about to be sounded . . . .*

Revelation 10:7

*The seventh angel then blew his trumpet . . . .*

Revelation 11:15

**How did the "trumpet call of the seventh angel" become the "trumpet of God"? Is God the seventh angel?**

Most certainly not! Revelation 8:2 tells us that the seventh angel stands before God. The Bible makes it clear that the *trumpet call of the seventh angel* is not the same as the *trumpet of God.* The *last trumpet* referred to in 1 Corinthians 15:52 is the same trumpet as in 1 Thessalonians 4:16, and is the trumpet of God. It is the last trumpet having to do with the earthbound Church. It is the trumpet that He sounds to summon us, His children, to move out, to meet His glorious Son in the air, and to be with Him forever.

Have you ever read the descriptions in Revelation of the people who go through the Tribulation Period, and have you ever wondered if those descriptions could ever apply to you?

*And the rest of humanity, who were not killed by these plagues, even then did not repent (out) of [the worship of] the works of their [own] hands, so as to cease paying homage to the demons and idols of gold and silver and bronze and stone and wood, which can neither see nor hear nor move.*

*And they did not repent (out) of their murders or their practice of magic (sorceries) or their sexual vice or their thefts.*

Revelation 9:20,21

*People were severely burned (scorched) by the fiery heat, and they reviled and blasphemed the name of God Who has control of these plagues, and they did not repent of their sins — felt no regret, contrition and compunction for their waywardness, refusing to amend their ways — to give Him glory.*

*Then the fifth angel emptied his bowl on the throne of the beast, and his kingdom was [plunged] in darkness, and people gnawed their tongues for the torment — of their excruciating distress and severe pain —*

*And blasphemed the God of heaven because of their anguish and their ulcers (sores), and they did not deplore their wicked deeds or repent — for what they had done.*

Revelation 16:9-11

If I saw these plagues happening to me, I'd be on my knees in a moment, full of repentance, and begging for the mercy of God. Are you any different in that respect? Not if you are a born-again child of God. Listen to what the Holy Spirit tells your spirit. If you are a born-again child of God, those preceding descriptions could not possibly apply to you. They apply to those who refuse to let the Blood of the Lamb wash them clean. They apply to the enemies of God, to those for whom He reserves His wrath.

But some people insist that everybody who is living during the Tribulation curses God because the Church has all been killed. Then they point to descriptions of martyred Tribulation saints and mistakenly identify them as the murdered Church. But if that is the case, how can the Rapture be a rapture of the living and the dead as the Word describes it (in two places)? It would have to be a rapture of the dead only.

I've heard people say, "Look, if God let His children go through World War

II, then He'll let His children go through the Tribulation."

Well, I don't have all the answers about the wars we've seen, but I know this: Nowhere does the Bible define World War II as an outpouring of the wrath of God; but it does define the Tribulation, very clearly, as a great outpouring of God's wrath. I choose to believe the Bible, and I will continue to trust in the power of the Blood of the Lamb of God.

*Therefore, since we are now justified — acquitted, made righteous and brought into right relationship with God — by Christ's blood, how much more [certain is it that] we shall be saved by Him from the indignation and wrath of God.*

*Romans* 5:9

**Is the Church "perfected" by tribulation?**

Without exception, the teachers of doom and gloom insist that persecution and tribulation are God's method for "perfecting" the Church, for "cleansing" it, and for making it ready for the (post-Tribulation) Rapture. They frequently use the diamond as an illustration, claiming that just as God forms the diamond under intense pressure, so He "perfects" the end-time Church.

You'll have to admit that it's an interesting theory, one that appeals to the flesh. However, this theory is not supported by the infallible Word of God. As a matter of fact, there isn't a shred of evidence to be found in God's Holy Word that tribulation is good for anything except patience. (Rom. 5:3.) But patience is also part of the fruit of the indwelling Holy Spirit. (Gal. 5:22.)

**How, then, does God perfect His Church? How does He cleanse it and purify it?**

The Bible is crystal clear on the subject. It's just like everything else in the victorious Christian life; it's man in partnership with God.

**God's Part**

First we must understand God's part in the cleansing, perfecting, and purifying of His Church.

Scripture reveals to us that the perfecting of the Church is a sovereign act of our Triune God. Father, Son, and Holy Spirit are all divinely involved in the perfecting of the Church.

For example, in the high priestly prayer that our Lord Jesus prayed to His Father in John, chapter 17, we read: *Sanctify them — purify, consecrate, separate them for Yourself, make them holy — by the Truth. Your Word is Truth* (v. 17).

Here Jesus asks His Father to sanctify and purify His Church by the Word of God. His prayer speaks of a perfection that is in the future; but our King also taught us that the perfection of the Church is a past accomplishment. Consider this:

*I am the True Vine and My Father is the Vinedresser.*

*Any branch in Me that does not bear fruit — that stops bearing — He cuts away (trims off, takes away). And He cleanses and repeatedly prunes every branch that continues to bear fruit, to make it bear more and richer and more excellent fruit.*

*You are cleansed and pruned already, because of the Word which I have given you — the teachings I have discussed with you.*

*John 15:1-3*

How very wonderful and comforting these scriptures are! They tell us that our Father in heaven cleanses and sanctifies and purifies us by the Word of God — not by persecution, trial, or tribulation; but by His infallible Word.

It therefore makes perfect sense when we flip over to 2 Timothy 3:16,17 and read in part: *Every Scripture is God-breathed . . . So that the man of God may be complete and proficient, well-fitted and thoroughly equipped for every good work.* God the Father has already done His part. He has already done what is necessary for our perfection — past, present, and future.

Paul wrote to the Philippian believers about God's ongoing work in perfecting His people:

*And I am convinced and sure of this very thing, that He Who began a good work in you will continue until the day of Jesus Christ — right up to the time of His return — developing [that good work] and perfecting and bringing it to full completion in you.*

*Philippians 1:6*

What God does to perfect His Church, He began when the Church was born on the day of Pentecost and continues right up to the "day of Christ." This is roughly a 2,000-year time span.

How, then, can people who claim to believe the Bible teach that God will use the seven-year Tribulation Period to perfect His Church? Furthermore, with regard to His Church, God is a God of peace, not a God of tribulation.

As Paul wrote to the believers at Thessalonica: *And may the God of peace Himself sanctify you through and through — that is, separate you from profane things, make you pure and wholly consecrated to God — and may your spirit and soul and body be preserved sound and complete [and found] blameless at the coming of our Lord Jesus Christ, the Messiah.*

*1 Thessalonians 5:23*

These last two scripture references make it crystal clear that the work which God does in perfecting and cleansing His Church is for the very purpose of making the Church ready for the Second Coming of our Lord.

As we all know, God treats all of His children the same. He doesn't perfect some by the Word and others by tribulation. He is not inconsistent. God is perfect, and His ways are perfect. That's why He never changes.

God the Son also purifies and perfects His Church: *For by a single offering He has forever completely cleansed and perfected those who are consecrated and made holy* (Heb. 10:14).

What could be clearer? *By a single offering* Jesus has forever cleansed and perfected us. Not by tribulation or persecution, but by the selfless sacrifice of the spotless Lamb of God.

And if we are forever cleansed, then who needs the future seven-year Tribulation? To teach that the Church is perfected by the Tribulation is to deny the power of God to purify us through His Word and through the Blood of His Beloved Son.

When God the Son perfects His Church, it is for the purpose of making us ready for the Second Coming; but which part of the Second Coming?

There is the appearing of Jesus, when He catches up the Church before the seven-year Tribulation, and there is the return of Jesus with His Church at the end of the seven-year Tribulation. Is God the Son making us ready for His *pre*-Tribulation appearing or His *post*-Tribulation return?

Paul's answer will make you leap for joy:

*Awaiting and looking for the [fulfillment, the realization of our] blessed hope, even the glorious appearing of our great God and Savior Christ Jesus, the Messiah, the Anointed One,*

*Who gave Himself on our behalf that He might redeem us (purchase our freedom) from all iniquity and purify for Himself a people — to be peculiarly His own . . . .*

*Titus 2:13,14*

Jesus Himself is purifying His Church to make Her ready for His pre-Tribulation appearing. Hallelujah!

The seven-year Tribulation has nothing to do with the ultimate perfection of the Church. As is taught in Ephesians 4:16, it is because of Him — not because of tribulation — that the whole Body grows to full maturity.

Paul told the Church at Rome that God the Holy Spirit was very much involved in their lives: *. . . I act in the priestly service of the Gospel (the good news) of God, in order that the sacrificial offering of the Gentiles may be acceptable [to God], consecrated and made holy by the Holy Spirit* (Rom. 15:16).

This teaches us that the present, day-in and day-out cleansing, purifying, and perfecting of the Church is a work of the Holy Spirit of God.

As you know, God the Holy Spirit works through our faith. *And He made no difference between us and them, but cleansed their hearts by faith . . .* (Acts 15:9). Faith in whom?

As Jesus said to Paul on the Damascus road, *. . . so that they may thus receive forgiveness and release from their sins and a place and portion among those who are consecrated and purified by faith in me* (Acts 26:18).

**Our Part**

Paul wrote to the Colossian church:

*Clothe yourselves therefore, as (God's own picked representatives,) His own chosen ones, [who are] purified and holy and well-beloved [by God Himself, by putting on behavior marked by] tenderhearted pity and mercy, kind feeling, a lowly opinion of yourselves, gentle ways, [and] patience — which is tireless, long-suffering and has the power to endure whatever comes, with good temper.*

*Colossians 3:12*

It appears that Paul is calling us to obedience and teaching us that we are purified through our obedience.

Peter agrees. In his first epistle he wrote, *Since by your obedience to the Truth through the [Holy] Spirit you have purified your hearts for the sincere affection of the brethren, [see that you] love one another fervently from a pure heart* (1 Pet. 1:22).

Both Paul and Peter find agreement in the Psalms: *Wherewith shall a young man cleanse his way? By taking heed and keeping watch [on himself] according to Your word [conforming his life to it]* (Ps. 119:9). Here we learn that, even before our Lord's sacrifice on the cross, God's method of cleansing us was always the same — through obedience to His Word.

Are you waiting for the glorious appearing of our Lord Jesus Christ? Then you'll love this scripture:

*. . . we know that when He comes and is manifested we shall [as God's children] resemble and be like Him, for we shall see Him just as He [really] is.*

*And every one who has this hope [resting] on Him cleanses (purifies) himself just as He is pure — chaste, undefiled, guiltless.*

1 John 3:2,3

There's as much of a need for you to go through the seven-year Tribulation as there is for Jesus Himself to go through it. Paul wrote:

*Furthermore, brethren, we beg and admonish you in [virtue of our union with] the Lord Jesus, that [you follow the instructions which] you learned from us about how you ought to walk so as to please and gratify God, as indeed you are doing; that you do so even more and more abundantly — attaining yet greater perfection in living this life.*

1 Thessalonians 4:1

The anonymous writer of Hebrews wrote, *Therefore let us go on and get past the elementary stage in the teachings and doctrine of Christ, the Messiah, advancing steadily toward the completeness and perfection that belongs to spiritual maturity . . .* (Heb. 6:1). How ridiculous it would be to assume that the only spiritually mature people are those who have suffered terribly during the seven-year Tribulation Period.

Second Timothy 2:21 teaches that we cleanse ourselves, not when we suffer tribulation, but when we willingly set ourselves apart from contaminating and corrupting influences.

Philippians 1:9,10 teaches that you may be untainted and pure by learning to sense, approve, and prize what is of God. And you'll find these things in the Church of Jesus Christ. That's why every born-again, Bible-believing child of God needs to be a part of a Bible-believing, Bible-teaching church.

*And His gifts were [varied; He Himself appointed and gave men to us,] some to be apostles (special messengers), some prophets (inspired preachers and expounders), some evangelists (preachers of the Gospel, traveling missionaries), some pastors (shepherds of His flock) and teachers.*

*His intention was the perfecting and the full equipping of the saints (His consecrated people) . . . .*

Ephesians 4:11,12

If you want to be perfected and made ready for the soon-coming Rapture of the Church, then you need to make yourself part of the Church. You need to put yourself under a Spirit-led pastor's authority. You need good teaching by anointed evangelists. (Read Hebrews 10:25.)

Conversely, to teach that the Church will be perfected by the seven-year Tribulation is the same as saying that you don't need the Church — a tragic mistake!

**A Final Note**

I am happily believing and trusting my Lord Jesus Christ to save me from everything defined by God's Word as the wrath of God. That includes the Tribulation. And I invite you, dear brothers and sisters in Christ, to share in His peace and joy.

Read your Bible (you'll discover many additional proofs) and discard your plans for going through the Tribulation. It is entirely inconsistent with the Word of God that the Church will go through the Tribulation.

Don't let Satan rob you any longer of the peace and joy that is yours by the authority of the Word of God.

See you up there!

Hilton Sutton

To receive Hilton Sutton's monthly publication, **UPDATE** write:

Mission To America
736 Wilson Road
Humble, Texas 77338